Media Persian

Books in the series

Media Persian
Dominic Parviz Brookshaw

Internet Arabic
Mourad Diouri

Security Arabic
Mark Evans

Media Arabic
2nd edition
Elisabeth Kendall

Intelligence Arabic
Julie C. Manning with Elisabeth Kendall

edinburghuniversitypress.com/series/emev

● Essential Middle Eastern Vocabularies ●

Media Persian

Dominic Parviz Brookshaw

EDINBURGH
University Press

Edinburgh University Press is one of the leading university presses in the UK. We publish academic books and journals in our selected subject areas across the humanities and social sciences, combining cutting-edge scholarship with high editorial and production values to produce academic works of lasting importance. For more information visit our website: edinburghuniversitypress.com

First published 2011
Reprinted 2014, 2019

Edinburgh University Press Ltd
The Tun – Holyrood Road, 12 (2f) Jackson's Entry
Edinburgh EH8 8PJ

Typeset in Times New Roman and
printed and bound in Great Britain

A CIP record for this book is available from the British Library

ISBN 978 0 7486 4100 0 (paperback)
ISBN 978 0 7486 4752 1 (webready PDF)
ISBN 978 0 7486 8875 3 (epub)

CONTENTS

USER GUIDE

To enhance your ability to recall the vocabulary and to pronounce it correctly, this book is accompanied by audio recordings of the entire contents of each chapter, recorded in both English and Persian term. The audio re-cordings can be downloaded from our website and are compatible with iPods and other devices.

To access the audio files, please follow the instructions on our website: https://edinburghuniversitypress. com/book-media-persian.html

Audio recordings

Main features

- Each Persian term is recorded with authentic native pronunciation at normal speed.
- Each Persian term is preceded by its equivalent in English.
- Each chapter is recorded as a single MP3 track (the track numbers correspond to the chapter numbers, e.g. Track 01 = Chapter 1).
- The audio files can be played on a computer or transferred to an MP3 device (e.g. iPod, mobile phone, etc.), enabling you to study on the move.

Tips

- Make sure that you engage actively with the audio recordings by repeating each Persian term during the pause.
- Pause the recording and challenge yourself to produce the Persian word before it is announced.

INTRODUCTION

The terminology used in the Persian-language media is constantly evolving; new words are being coined and foreign words are adapted and adopted into the language. This is why a quick-fix vocabulary of essential media Persian is vital to learners wishing to tap into the ever-growing multi-media world of Persian-language satellite TV, radio, websites, blogs and print media both inside and outside Iran. Much of the vocabulary included in this book cannot be found in even the latest Persian dictionaries. Although focused on the Iranian form of Persian (Farsi), this book will prove just as useful to those wishing to understand broadcasting and writing in Afghan Persian (Dari). Every effort has been made to ensure that the vocabulary listed here is that currently used in the Persian-language media, and that it is as up-to-date as possible.

This book is divided into thirteen chapters covering a wide range of topics frequently reported in the Persian media: General; Politics and Government; Elections; Conflict and Security; Law and Order; Human Rights; Economics; Trade and Industry; Science and Technology; Energy; Environment; Aid and Development; and Culture and Sport. A great deal of thought has gone into how best to divide vocabulary between chapters which overlap in terms of subject matter (e.g. Law and Order and Human Rights), and every effort has been made to avoid any repetition of vocabulary between chapters, except where absolutely necessary due to nuances in meaning and usage. The vocabulary featured here is not exhaustive, but rather it is core, and provides a solid basis for undergraduates, postgraduates, journalists, diplomats, politicians, business people and others wishing to read, write, speak, listen to, and translate media Persian.

Some notes on the formal presentation

The vocabulary in each chapter (bar the General chapter) is arranged with particular emphasis on the etymology and meaning of words. Strict alphabetical ordering has been avoided on the whole since this is counter-productive to learning vocabulary lists. Within each chapter vocabulary items are grouped in smaller, untitled sub-sections by topic, which means that the book can be used easily as a reference tool, although it is not aimed at replacing the use of dictionaries altogether. Users will detect the internal logic of the ordering of vocabulary items.

The Arabic plural has been given in brackets after those nouns for which it is commonly used. All animate nouns in Persian can be pluralised by adding ان- (or گان- if the noun ends in silent ه). All other nouns can be pluralised by simply adding

Short vowels have not been indicated, since they do not commonly appear in printed and online media Persian texts. The user should refer to the online audio files for guidance on received pronunciation.

The *ezāfe* has been shown throughout to aid the correct reading and oral use of phrases where it appears in Persian.

Not all transitive/intransitive forms of verbs have been given, nor have all adjectival forms, only those encountered most commonly. The following descriptors have been added wherever ambiguity might exist: (adj.) adjective; (n.) noun; (v.i.) intransitive verb; (v.t.) transitive verb.

I would like to thank Elisabeth Kendall, Pouneh Shabani Jadidi, and Naseem Alizadeh for their comments on an earlier draft of this book.

Dominic Parviz Brookshaw
Manchester
August 2010

1. GENERAL

رسانه ها	the media
رسانه های گروهی	mass media
چند رسانه ای	multi-media
مطبوعات	the press
مطبوعاتی	press (adj.)
اطلاعیهٔ مطبوعاتی	press release
اعلامیه، بیانیه	statement
کنفرانس ِ مطبوعاتی	press conference
سخنگوی مطبوعاتی	press spokesperson
روابط ِ عمومی	public relations
روزنامه	newspaper
روزنامه نگار	print journalist
روزنامه نگاری	print journalism
خبر (اخبار)	news
تیتر ِ اخبار	news headlines
خبررسان	newscaster

خبرگزار	correspondent
خبرگزاری	news agency
خبرنگار	journalist
خبریابی	news gathering
اتاق ِ خبر	newsroom
کنفرانس ِ خبری	news conference
گزارش	report
گزارش دادن	to report
گزارش شده	reported
گزارشگر	reporter
تحلیل	analysis
تحلیل کردن	to analyse
تحلیلگر	analyst
مفسّر (مفسّرین)	commentator
برنامه	programme
تلویزیون ِ ماهواره ای	satellite television
کانال	channel
مجری	presenter

رادیوِ دیجیتالی	digital radio
گویندۀ رادیو	radio presenter
پخش کردن	to broadcast
تهیه کننده	producer
تهیه کردن	to produce
زنده	live
مصاحبه	interview
مصاحبه شونده	interviewee
مصاحبه کردن با	to interview
مصاحبه گر	interviewer
بازنویسی کردن	to rewrite
پیش نویس	draft
تیراژ	print run
چاپ کردن، منتشر کردن	to publish
ناشر	publisher
ستون	column
ستون نویس	columnist
سرخط	header

عنوان، تیتر	title
سر دبیر	editor (of a newspaper)
سر دبیری کردن	to edit (a newspaper)
سر مقاله	editorial
ویراستاری کردن	to edit
ویراستار	editor
فصلنامه	periodical
متن (متون)	text
مجله (مجلات)	journal; magazine
مطلب (مطالب)	story
موضوع (موضوعات)	topic
مقاله (مقالات)	article; essay
منبع (منابع)	source
منابع ِ معتبر	reliable sources
نظر	opinion
نقطه نظر	point of view

ايرنا (خبرگزاری ِ جمهوری ِ اسلامی ِ ايران)	IRNA (Islamic Republic News Agency)
ايسنا (خبرگزاری ِ دانشجويان ِ ايران)	ISNA (Iranian Students' News Agency)
بی بی سی	BBC (British Broadcasting Corporation)
راديو فردا	Radio Farda
صدا و سيمای جمهوری ِ اسلامی ِ ايران	IRIB (Islamic Republic of Iran Broadcasting)
صدای آمريکا	Voice of America
صدای اسرائيل	Voice of Israel
ابراز کردن	to express
ابراز ِ نگرانی کردن	to express anxiety
اتفاق افتادن	to happen
ادّعا کردن	to assert, to claim
اذعان کردن	to acknowledge
ارائه کردن	to present (e.g. a view)

اشاره کردن به	to point to; to indicate
اظهار داشتن	to express
اظهار نظر کردن	to express an opinion
اعتراف کردن	to admit
اعلام کردن	to announce
افزایش دادن	to increase (v.t.)
افزایش یافتن	to increase (v.i.)
افزودن	to add
انتقاد کردن	to criticise
ایجاد کردن	to create
باعثِ ... شدن	to cause
بحث کردن	to discuss
برخورد کردن با	to encounter
برگزار کردن	to hold (an event)
به تعویق افتادن	to be delayed

به خطر انداختن	to jeopardise
به شکست انجامیدن	to fail (e.g. talks)
بیان کردن	to express
بیانگر ِ چیزی بودن	to be indicative of
پایان دادن به	to put an end to
پس گرفتن	to retract
پیش بینی کردن	to predict
پیشنهاد کردن	to suggest
پیوستن به	to join
تأکید کردن بر	to emphasise; to stress
تجدید ِ نظر کردن	to rethink
تحت ِ فشار بودن	to be under pressure
تحت ِ فشار قرار دادن	to put under pressure
تفسیر کردن	to interpret (events)
تلویحاً گفتن	to allude to
جلوگیری کردن از	to prevent

خواستار ِ چیزی شدن	to seek
خواهان ِ چیزی بودن	to ask for
دانستن	to consider
در نظر گرفتن	to take into consideration
درز کردن	to leak (e.g. information)
دیدار کردن با	to meet with
رد کردن	to refute; to reject
روشن کردن	to clarify
شک کردن در	to doubt
صحّت ِ چیزی را مورد تردید قرار دادن	to doubt the validity of something
عنوان کردن	to raise (e.g. an issue)
فاش کردن	to disclose
فرض کردن	to hypothesise
قول دادن	to pledge
کاهش دادن	to decrease (v.t.)

کاهش یافتن	to decrease (v.i.)
کسی را مسئول دانستن	to consider someone responsible
گمراه کردن	to mislead
لغو کردن	to cancel
لکه دار کردن	to tarnish
مخالفت کردن با	to oppose
مشخّص کردن	to pinpoint
مطرح کردن	to put forward
ملاقات کردن با	to meet
منجر شدن به	to lead to
موفق شدن	to succeed
نادیده گرفتن	to ignore
ناشی شدن از	to arise out of
نقش بازی کردن	to play a role
نقلِ قول کردن	to quote
هدف قرار دادن	to target

هشدار دادن به	to warn
ادّعا می شود که ...	it is alleged that
انتظار می رود که ...	it is expected that
این در حالیست که ...	this comes at a time when
به این شرط که ...	on the condition that
به درخواست ِ ...	at the request of
به عنوان ِ ...	as
پیش بینی می شود که ...	it is predicted that
تا آنجایی که ...	so far as
در آستانهٔ ...	on the eve of
در آینده ای نه چندان دور	in the not so distant future
در ارتباط با ...	in relation to
در پی ِ ...	in the wake of
در طی ِ چند سال اخیر	over the past few years
در این مورد	in this regard

در جواب ِ ...	in answer to
در حالیکه ...	whereas
در زمینهٔ ...	in the field of
در سطح ِ جهانی	worldwide
در شرایط ِ فعلی	in the present circumstances
طی ِ چند روز ِ آینده	over the next few days
نظر به اینکه ...	in view of the fact that
اجتناب ناپذیر	inevitable
انجام شدنی	doable
انعطاف ناپذیر	inflexible
انکار ناپذیر	undeniable
با تجربه	experienced
با نفوذ	influential
باور نکردنی	unbelievable
بحث برانگیز	controversial
بدون ِ نتیجهٔ قطعی	indecisive

بلند مدّت	long-term
بی اساس	baseless
بی سابقه	unprecedented
بی قید و شرط	unequivocal
پی در پی	consecutive
پیچیده	complex
پیش بینی نشده	unanticipated
تأسّف آور	regrettable
تأیید نشده	unconfirmed
تصوّر کردنی	conceivable
خستگی ناپذیر	tireless
دست یافتنی	achievable
دوررس	far-reaching
رد کردنی	refutable
رک	frank
سازنده	constructive
سؤال بر انگیز	questionable
صریح	outspoken

ضمنی	implied
عملی	doable; practical
غیر ِ قابل ِ پیش بینی	unpredictable
غیر ِ قابل ِ فهم	unintelligible
غیر ِ قابل ِ قبول	unacceptable
غیر ِ منتظره	unexpected
فرضی	hypothetical
قابل ِ اعتماد	reliable
قریب الوقوع	imminent
قطعی	definite
کلیدی	key
کوتاه مدّت	short-term
مبهم	vague
محوری	pivotal
مطلع	informed
ملموس	tangible
مساعد	favourable
موفق	successful

نامساعد	unfavourable
نامعلوم	unclear
ناموفق	unsuccessful
نمادین	symbolic
هدفمند	purposeful
همزمان	concurrent

2. POLITICS & GOVERNMENT

سياست	politics; policy
سياستِ ارضا	appeasement
سياست بازى	politicking
سياستِ زور	power politics
سياست گذار	policy-maker
سياست گذارى	policy-making
سياست مدار	politician
سياسى	political
سياسى شدن	politicisation
سياسى كردن	to politicise
از نظرِ سياسى	politically
پهنهٔ سياسى	political spectrum
سيستمِ سياسى	political system
علومِ سياسى	political science
غيرِ سياسى	non-political
بى طرف	neutral

آنارشیست	anarchist (n.)
آنارشیسم	anarchism
استبداد	despotism
استعمارگر	colonialist (n.)
استعمارگری	colonialism
اسلامگرا	Islamist (n.)
اسلامگرایی	Islamism
اصلاح طلب	reformist (n.)
اصلاح طلبی	reformism
اصولگرا	fundamentalist (n.)
اصولگرایی	fundamentalism
اعتدالی	moderate (adj.)
معتدل (معتدلین)	moderate (n.)
افراط گرا	extremist (n.)
افراط گرایی	extremism
الیگارشی	oligarchy
امپریالیست	imperialist (n.)
امپریالیسم	imperialism

انزوا طلب	isolationist (n.)
انزوا طلبی	isolationism
ایدآلیسم	idealism
آرمان گرا	idealist
ایدئولوژی	ideology
ایدئولوژیک	ideological
تندرو	hard-liner
توتالیتر	totalitarian (adj.)
توتالیتریسم	totalitarianism
جدایی طلب	separatist (n.)
جدایی طلبی	separatism
چپگرا	leftist (adj. and n.)
چپگرایی	leftism
چند فرهنگی گرایی	multiculturalism
دموکراتیک	democratic
دموکراسی	democracy
دیکتاتور	dictator
دیکتاتوری	dictatorship

رادیکال	radical
رلدیکالیسم	radicalism
راستگرا	right-wing
سرمایه دار	capitalist (n.)
سرمایه داری	capitalism
سکولار	secular
سکولاریست	secularist
سکولاریسم	secularism
سلطنت	monarchy
سلطنت مشروطه	constitutional monarchy
سلطنت طلب	royalist (n.)
سلطنت طلبی	monarchism
سوسیالیست	socialist (n.)
سوسیالیسم	socialism
صهیونیست	Zionist (n.)
صهیونیسم	Zionism
عملگرا	pragmatist (n.)

عملگرایی	pragmatism
فاشیشت	fascist (n.)
فاشیستی	fascist (adj.)
فاشیسم	fascism
فدرال	federal
فدرالیست	federalist (n.)
فدرالیسم	federalism
فرصت طلب	opportunist
فرطت طلبی	opportunism
قوم گرایی	tribalism
کثرت گرایی	pluralism
کمونیست	communist (n.)
کمونیسم	communism
لیبرالیست	liberalist
لیبرالیسم	liberalism
مائوئیست	Maoist (n.)
مائوئیسم	Maoism
مارکسیست	Marxist (n.)

ماركسيسم	Marxism
محافظه کار	conservative
محافظه کاری	conservatism
مشروطه خواه	constitutionalist (n.)
مشروطه خواهی	constitutionalism
ملی گرا	nationalist (n.)
ملی گرایی	nationalism
نازی	Nazi
نازیسم	Nazism
نئونازیسم	neo-Nazism
نو محافظه کار	neo-conservative
نو محافظه کاری	neo-conservatism
واقع بین	realist (n.)
واقع بینی	realism
وطن پرست	patriot
وطن پرستی	patriotism
حزب (احزاب)	political party
حزب ِ اقلیت	minority party

حزب ِ اکثریت	majority party
حزب بازی	party politics
حزب ِ جمهوری خواه	Republican Party
حزب ِ دموکرات	Democratic Party
حزب ِ کارگر	Labour Party
حزب ِ لیبرال دموکرات	Liberal Democrats
حزب ِ محافظه کار	Conservative Party
حزب ِ مخالف	opposition party
خط ِ مشی ِ حزب	party line
تک حزبی	single-party
چند حزبی	multi-party
دو حزبی	bipartisan
جناح	wing
دسته	faction
عضو (اعضا)	member
عضو ِ ... شدن	to become a member of
عضویت	membership

اعضای وفادار ِ حزب	the party faithful
پارلمان	parliament
پارلمان ِ معلق	hung parliament
پارلمان ِ اروپا	The European Parliament
پارلمانی	parliamentary
نماینده، وکیل (وکلاء)	member (of parliament)
مجلس	Majlis; parliament
مجلس ِ شورای ِ اسلامی	Islamic Consultative Assembly
رئیس ِ مجلس	speaker of the parliament
مجلس ِ عوام	House of Commons
مجلس ِ اعیان	House of Lords
مجلس ِ خبرگان	Council of Experts
سنا	The Senate
سناتور	Senator
کنگره	Congress

عضو ِ کنگره	member of Congress
انحلال	dissolution
اکثریت ِ مطلق	overall majority
دوره	term
اجلاس	meeting
اجلاس ِ سران	summit
جلسه (جلسات)	meeting; session
جلسهٔ غیر ِ علنی	closed session
رئیس ِ جلسه	chairperson
دستور ِ جلسه	agenda
دیدار	meeting; visit
دیدار کردن با	to meet with
سفر ِ رسمی	official visit
سمینار	seminar
شورا	council
شورای نگهبان	Guardian Council

مجمع ِ تشخیص ِ مصلحت ِ نظام	Expediency Council
مجمع ِ عمومی ِ سالانه	AGM (Annual General Meeting)
میزگرد	roundtable
نشست	session
کمیته	committee
کمیسیون	commission
کنفرانس، همایش	conference
کنگره	congress
گرد هم آیی	gathering; meeting
حکومت	government
حکومتی	governmental
حکومت ِ ائتلافی	coalition government
حکومت ِ فدرال	federal government
حکومت ِ دینی	theocracy
حکومت کردن	to govern

حکم راندن	to rule
حکمرانی	governance
دولت	government; state
دولت ِ اقلیت	minority government
دولت ِ مرکزی	central government
دولتی	governmental; state (adj.)
سخنگوی دولت	government spokesperson
کارمند ِ دولت	civil servant
کشور	country; state
کشور ِ عضو	member state
کشور ِ میزبان	host country
قدرت	power
ابر قدرت	superpower
انتقال ِ قدرت	transfer of power
تقسیم ِ قدرت	power-sharing
پایگاه ِ قدرت	power base

به قدرت رسیدن	to come to power
کناره گیری کردن	to step aside
بر کنار کردن	to oust
معزول کردن	to depose
رژیم	regime
تغییرِ رژیم	regime change
استقلال	independence
مستقل	independent
خودمختار	autonomous
خودمختاری	autonomy, self-rule
دستور	order
دستور دادن	to order
رهبر	leader
رهبرِ معظم	Supreme Leader
رهبری	leadership
رهنمود	directive
سران	heads of state
فرمان (فرامین)	decree

فرمانروا	ruler
فرمانروایی کردن بر	to rule over
سلسلۀ مراتب	hierarchy
شایسته سالاری	meritocracy
نخبه سالاری	elitism
شهردار	mayor
مشاور	adviser; aide
همتا	counterpart
ارشد	senior
عالی رتبه	high-ranking
مقامات	authorities; officials
مقامات ِ بلندپایه	high-ranking officials
غیر ِ متعهّد	non-aligned
نظام	political system
نظم ِ نوین ِ جهانی	New World Order
تابع (اتباع)	national (n.)
تابعیت، ملیّت	nationality

جامعه (جوامع)	community; society
جامعهٔ بین المللی	The International Community
جامعهٔ مدنی	civil society
رعیّت (رعایا)	subject
شهروند	citizen
شهروندی	citizenship
مردم	the people
تودهٔ مردم	the masses
عموم ِ مردم	the public
هموطن	compatriot
جمهوری	republic
جمهوری ِ اسلامی ِ ایران	Islamic Republic of Iran
ریاست ِ جمهوری	presidency
(مربوط به) ریاست ِ جمهوری	presidential
رئیس جمهور	president
رئیس جمهور ِ سابق	former president

رئیس جمهور ِ منتخب	president-elect
معاون ِ رئیس جمهور	vice-president
کاخ ِ ریاست ِ جمهوری	presidential palace
کاخ ِ سفید	The White House
نخست وزیر	prime minister
معاون ِ نخست وزیر	deputy prime minister
وزیر (وزراء)	minister
معاون ِ وزیر	deputy minister
وزارت	ministry
وزارت خانه	ministry (building)
وزارتی	ministerial
کابینه	cabinet
کابینهٔ حزب ِ مخالف	shadow cabinet
ترمیم ِ کابینه	cabinet reshuffle
تعیین کردن	to appoint
منصوب شدن	to be appointed
انتصاب	appointment

دیپلمات	diplomat
دیپلماتیک	diplomatic
دیپلماسی	diplomacy
مصونیت ِ دیپلماتیک	diplomatic immunity
روابط ِ دیپلماتیک	diplomatic relations
سفارت	embassy
سفارت خانه	embassy (building)
سفیر (سفراء)	ambassador
کنسول	consul
کنسولگری	consulate
سازمان ِ ملل ِ متحد، سازمان ِ ملل، ملل ِ متحد	UN, United Nations
منشور ِ سازمان ِ ملل	UN charter
دبیر ِ کل	Secretary-General
دبیرخانه	secretariat
رأی ِ منفی	veto
شورای امنیت	Security Council

عضو ِ دائمی	permanent member
فرستادهٔ ویژه	special envoy
قطعنامه	resolution
کمیسر ِ عالی	high commissioner
کمیسریای عالی	high commission
مجمع ِ عمومی	General Assembly
یونسکو (سازمان ِ آموزشی، علمی و فرهنگی ِ ملل متحد)	UNESCO (United Nations Educational, Scientific and Cultural Organization)
یونیسف (صندوق ِ کودکان ِ ملل ِ متحد)	UNICEF (United Nations Children's Fund)
اتحادیهٔ آفریقا	African Union
اتحادیهٔ اروپا	The European Union
اتحادیهٔ عرب	The Arab League
اتحادیهٔ کشورهای مستقل ِ همسود	CIS (Commonwealth of Independent States)

اتحادیهٔ کشورهای جنوب شرقی ِ آسیا	ASEAN (The Association of Southeast Asian Nations)
سازمان ِ کنفرانس ِ اسلامی	OIC (Organization of the Islamic Conference)
شورای همکاری ِ خلیج ِ فارس	GCC (Gulf Cooperation Council)
کشورهای مشترک المنافع	The Commonwealth
کمیسیون ِ اروپا	European Commission
گروه ِ هفت	G7
گروه ِ بیست	G20
اعتراض (اعتراضات)	protest
اعتراض کردن	to protest
اعتصاب ِ غذا	hunger strike
اعتصاب ِ نشسته	sit-in
تظاهرات	demonstration
تظاهرات کردن	to demonstrate

تظاهرکننده	demonstrator
نافرمانی مدنی	civil disobedience
جنبش	movement
جنبش ِ اجتماعی	social movement
جنبش ِ زنان	the women's movement
جنبش ِ سبز	The Green Movement
راه پیمایی	street protest
شعار	slogan
فعّال ِ سیاسی	political activist
بی تفاوتی ِ سیاسی	political apathy
گروه ِ فشار	pressure group

3. ELECTIONS

انتخابات	elections
انتخابات ِ ریاست ِ جمهوری	presidential elections
انتخابات ِ سراسری	nationwide elections
انتخابات ِ محلی	local elections
انتخابات ِ میان دوره ای	mid-term elections
نتایج ِ انتخابات	election results
انتخاب شدن	to be elected
انتخاب کردن	to elect
انتخاب ِ مجدّد	re-election
تبلیغات ِ انتخاباتی	electioneering
دوباره انتخاب شدن	to be re-elected
دوباره انتخاب کردن	to re-elect
حوزهٔ انتخاباتی	constituency
کمیسیون ِ انتخاباتی	electoral commission
مبارز	campaigner

مبارزهٔ انتخاباتی	election campaign
مانیفیست	manifesto
ناظر ِ انتخاباتی	election monitor
نظارت بر انتخابات	election monitoring
رأی (آراء)	vote
صندوق ِ رأی	ballot box
رأی ِ اعتماد	vote of confidence
رأی دادن به	to vote for
رأی دهنده	voter
رأی دهندگان	electorate
رأی شماری	vote-counting
رأی ِ عدم ِ اعتماد	vote of no confidence
رأی علیهِ ... دادن	to vote against
رأی ِ مثبت دادن به	to vote in favour of
رأی ِ مخفی	secret ballot
چیزی را به رأی گذاشتن	to put something to the vote
رأی گرفتن	to receive votes

رأی گیری	ballot; voting
اتاقکِ رأی گیری	voting booth
برگۀ رأی گیری	ballot paper
تقلب در رأی گیری	vote-rigging
حوزۀ رأی گیری	voting station
نامزد، کاندیدا	candidate
نامزدی	candidacy
نامزد بودن	to stand for election
نامزد کردن	to nominate
ردِّ صلاحیت	de-selection
حامی	supporter
حمایت کردن از	to support
نظرسنج	pollster
نظرسنجی	opinion poll
آراءِ عمومی	public opinion
آمار	statistics
رفراندوم، همه پرسی	referendum

4. CONFLICT & SECURITY

اغتشاش (اغتشاشات)	disturbance
انتقام	revenge
انتقام گرفتن	to take revenge
تجاوز ِ نظامی	military invasion
تجاوز کردن به	to invade
تحریک	provocation
تحریک کردن	to provoke
تخریب کردن	to destroy
تسخیر کردن	to capture (territory)
تعرّض	aggression
تنش	tension
توسل به زور	use of force
توطئه	conspiracy
تهدید (تهدیدات)	threat
تهدید کردن	to threaten

تهدید آمیز	threatening
حمله (حملات)	attack
حمله کردن	to attack
حمله کننده	attacker
خشن	violent
خشونت	violence
خونریزی	bloodshed
درگیری	clash
زد و خورد	scuffle
شدت گرفتن	to escalate
شدت گیری	escalation
کش مکش	conflict; skirmish
مبارزه کردن با	to combat
محاصره	blockade; siege
مناقشه	dispute
نابود کردن	to annihilate
نجات دادن	to rescue; to save
نزاع	dispute; quarrel

هجوم	attack; raid
اشغال	occupation
اشغال کردن	to occupy
اشغالگر	occupier
اشغالی	occupied
اراضی ِ اشغالی	The Occupied Territories
شهرک ِ یهودی نشین	Jewish settlement
جنگ	war
در حال ِ جنگ	at war
جنگنده	fighter
جنگیدن	to fight
جنگ ِ جهانی	world war
جنگ ِ تحمیلی	The Imposed War (the Iran–Iraq War)
جنگ ِ داخلی	civil war
جنگ ِ سرد	The Cold War
جنگ ِ عادلانه	just war

اعلان ِ جنگ کردن	to declare war
جنگ سالار	warlord
جنایت ِ جنگی	war crime
محکمهٔ جنایات ِ جنگی	war crimes tribunal
جنایتکار ِ جنگی	war criminal
جنایت ِ علیه ِ بشریت	crime against humanity
اسیر (اسراء)	prisoner of war
جانباز	war wounded
خط ِ مقدم	frontline
دشمن	enemy
همدست ِ دشمن	collaborator
رزمنده	war veteran
شهید (شهداء)	martyr; war dead
تسلیم	surrender
تسلیم شدن	to surrender
پیروزی	victory
دفاع	defence

دفاع ِ مقدّس	Sacred Defence
شکست	defeat
شکست خوردن	to be defeated
شکست دادن	to defeat
آسیب	injury; damage
آسیب دیدن	to be injured
پاکسازی ِ نژادی	ethnic cleansing
قتل ِ عام	mass killing
نژادکشی، قوم کشی	genocide
تلفات	loss of life
زخمی	injured
زخمی شدن	to be injured
قربانی	victim
کشتار	killing
کشته	killed
شمار ِ کشته شدگان	death toll
مجروح (مجروحین)	wounded
مجروح شدن	to be wounded

مرگبار	deadly
ارتش	army
ارتش ِ اشغالگر	occupying army
اردوگاه	army camp
پادگان	barracks
استراتژی	strategy
بسیج	mobilisation; Basij
تاکتیک	tactic
تیمسار	general
خدمت ِ نظام وظیفه، سربازی	military service
حملۀ زمینی	ground attack
درجه	rank
درجه دار	non-commissioned officer
سپاه ِ پاسداران	Revolutionary Guard
ستاد	headquarters
ستاد ِ ارتش	army staff

سرباز ِ وظیفه	conscript
عقب نشینی	withdrawal
عملیات	operations
فراری	deserter
فرمانده	commander
فرماندهٔ کل ِ قوا	commander-in-chief
گشت	patrol
مانور	manoeuvre
متفقین	allies
ناتو (سازمان ِ پیمان ِ آتلانتیک ِ شمالی)	NATO (North Atlantic Treaty Organization)
نظامی	military
نظامی سازی	militarisation
غیر ِ نظامی سازی	demilitarisation
نظامی کردن	to militarise
نظامی گرایی	militarism
منطقهٔ نظامی	militarised zone

غیر ِ نظامی	civilian
نیروها	forces
نیروهای احتیاط	reserves
نیروهای مسلح	armed forces
نیروی انتظامی	police
نیروی دریایی	navy
نیروی هوایی	air force
پایگاه ِ هوایی	airbase
سلاح ها، اسلحه	arms; weapons
سلاح های اتمی	nuclear weapons
سلاح های شیمیایی	chemical weapons
سلاح های کشتار ِ جمعی	WMD (weapons of mass destruction)
خلع ِ سلاح	disarmament
خلع ِ سلاح های اتمی	nuclear disarmament
منع ِ گسترش ِ سلاح های اتمی	nuclear non-proliferation
مسابقۀ تسلیحاتی	arms race

مسلح	armed
غیر ِ مسلح	unarmed
انفجار (انفجارات)	explosion
مواد ِ منفجره	explosives
بمب	bomb
بمب خنثی کردن	to defuse a bomb
بمب ِ خوشه ای	cluster bomb
بمب ِ کنار ِ جاده ای	roadside bomb
خودروی حاوی ِ بمب	car bomb
محل ِ انفجار ِ بمب	bombsite
بمباران	bombardment
بمباران کردن	to bomb (aerial)
بمبگذار	bomber
بمبگذار ِ انتحاری	suicide bomber
بمبگذاری	bombing
بمبگذاری ِ انتحاری	suicide bombing
تیراندازی	shooting
تیرادازی کردن	to shoot

تانک	tank
خمپاره	mortar
رادار	radar
زیر دریایی	submarine
مسلسل	machine gun
منطقۀ پرواز ممنوع	no-fly zone
موشک	missile
موشک ِ دوربرد	long-range missile
موشک ِ ضد ِ هوایی	anti-aircraft missile
موشک ِ کوتاه برد	short-range missile
مهمّات	ammunition
مین	land mine
مین یاب	mine detector
میدان ِ مین	minefield
نارنجک	hand grenade
ناو ِ جنگی	warship
هواپیمای بدون ِ سرنشین	unmanned aircraft
انقلاب	revolution

انقلاب ِ اسلامی	Islamic Revolution
انقلاب ِ فرهنگی	cultural revolution
انقلاب ِ مخملی	velvet revolution
انقلاب ِ مشروطه	Constitutional Revolution
انقلابی (انقلابیون)	revolutionary
کودتا	coup
بر انداختن	to overthrow
براندازی	overthrow
بی ثباتی	instability
فروپاشی	collapse
فروپاشیدن	to collapse
شورش	revolt, rebellion; insurgency; riot
شورشی	rebel; insurgent; rioter
شورشی را فروخواباندن	to put down a revolt
پلیس ِ ضد ِ شورش	riot police
ظلم کردن به	to oppress

سرکوب کردن	to suppress
سرکوبگر	repressive
قیام	uprising
گاز ِ اشک آور	tear gas
مبارز ِ آزادی خواه	freedom fighter
شبه ِ نظامیان	militia
ارتش ِ جمهوری خواه ِ ایرلند	IRA (Irish Republican Army)
حزب الله	Hezbollah
طالبان	Taliban
مجاهدین	Mujahideen
سازمان ِ مجاهدین ِ خلق	MKO (Mojahedin-e Khalq Organization)
مقاومت	resistance
مقاومت ِ مسلحانه	armed resistance
مقاومت کردن	to resist
نا آرامی	unrest

نارضایتی	discontent
آدم ربا	kidnapper
آدم ربایی	kidnapping
القاعده	Al-Qaeda
ترور	assassination
ترور کردن	to assassinate
تروریست	terrorist
گروه ِ تروریستی	terrorist group
تروریسم	terrorism
تروریسم ِ دولتی	state terrorism
جنگ علیه ِ تروریسم	War on Terror
گروگان	hostage
گروگان گرفتن	to take hostage
گروگان گیری	hostage taking
محور ِ شرارت	Axis of Evil
هواپیما ربا	hijacker
هواپیما ربایی	hijacking
امنیت	security (n.)

امنیت ِ جمعی	collective security
امنیت ِ ملی	national security
امنیتی	security (adj.)
مخاطرۀ امنیتی	security risk
نیروهای امنیتی	security forces
انگشت نگاری	finger printing
کارت ِ شناسایی	identity card
ایست ِ بازرسی	check point
حالت ِ اضطراری	state of emergency
خاموشی	curfew
پلیس ِ مخفی	secret police
جاسوس	spy
جاسوس ِ دوجانبه	double agent
جاسوسی	espionage
سازمان ِ اطلاعات	intelligence agency
لباس شخصی	plain clothes
مأمور ِ مخفی	secret agent
نظارت	surveillance

بن بست	impasse
آتش بس	ceasefire
آرام	calm (adj.)
آرامش	calm (n.)
آشتی	reconciliation
حقیقت و آشتی	truth and reconciliation
آشتی کردن	to make peace
حل ِ اختلاف	conflict resolution
حل ِ درگیری	dispute resolution
حل کردن	to resolve; to solve
صلح	peace
صلح آمیز، مسالمت آمیز	peaceful
جنبش ِ صلح	peace movement
روند ِ صلح	peace process
سپاه ِ صلح	The Peace Corps
نیروی حافظ ِ صلح	peace-keeping force
عدم ِ خشونت	non-violence

پیمان	agreement; pact
پیمان بستن	to enter into an agreement
توافق	agreement
به توافق رسیدن	to reach an agreement
عهدنامه	treaty
قرارداد	agreement
قرارداد ِ دوجانبه	bilateral agreement
امضا کننده	signatory
امضا کردن	to sign
گفتگو	dialogue
گفتگوی تمدن ها	Dialogue Among Civilizations
گفتگو ها	talks
مذاکرات	negotiations
مذاکرات ِ دوجانبه	bilateral negotiations

مذاکره کننده	negotiator
مذاکره کردن	to negotiate
میز ِ مذاکره	negotiation table
داوری	arbitration
میانجی گری	mediation

5. LAW & ORDER

قانون (قوانین)	law
قانونیت	legality
قوانین و مقررات	rules and regulations
قانونی	legal
غیر ِ قانونی	illegal
قانونی کردن	to legalise
قانون را نقض کردن	to break the law
مطیع ِ قانون	law-abiding
قانون ِ اساسی	constitution
مبتنی بر قانون ِ اساسی	constitutional
مغایر ِ قانون ِ اساسی	unconstitutional
قانون ِ جزایی	penal law
قانون ِ جنایی	criminal law
قانون ِ مجازات ِ عمومی	penal code
قانون مدنی	civil law

تدوین ِ قوانین	codification
لایحهٔ قانونی	bill
ماده	article (of law)
اختیار ِ قانونی	jurisdiction
پیگرد ِ قانونی	prosecution
حاکمیت ِ قانون	rule of law
مهلت ِ قانونی	moratorium
حقوق ِ بین المللی	international law
قانون گذاشتن	to legislate
قانونگذار	legislator
قانونگذاری	legislation
(مربوط به) قانونگذاری	legislative (adj.)
عرف	common law
شرع	religious law
شریعت	Sharia (Islamic law)
مشروع	legitimate
مشروعیت	legitimacy
نا مشروع	illegitimate

دادگاه	court of law
جلسهٔ دادگاه	hearing
دادگاه ِ استیناف	court of appeal
دادگاه ِ انقلاب	revolutionary court
دادگاه ِ عالی	High Court
دیوان ِ بین المللی ِ دادگستری	International Court of Justice
دیوان ِ بین المللی ِ کیفری	International Criminal Court
دادخواهی	lawsuit
دادرسی	legal procedure
دادستان	public prosecutor
دادگستری، عدالت	justice
وزارت ِ دادگستری	Ministry of Justice
بی عدالتی	injustice
عادلانه	just
غیر ِ عادلانه	unjust
محاکمه	trial

محاکمه شدن	to be tried
محاکمه کردن	to try
محکوم کردن	to convict
حکم	sentence; verdict
حکمِ اعدام	death sentence
حکمِ برائت	verdict of not guilty
حکم صادر کردن	to issue a verdict
حکمِ محکومیت	verdict of guilty
مقصّر دانستن	to find guilty
عفو	pardon
قاضی	judge
قوۀ قضائیه	judiciary
وکیل (وکلاء)	lawyer
هیئتِ منصفه	jury
شاکی	plaintiff
مدّعی	claimant
مظنون	suspect
شاهد (شهود)	witness

شاهد ِ عینی	eye witness
شهادت	testimony
شهادت دادن	to testify
سوگند خوردن	to swear an oath
اتهام (اتهامات)	charge
متهم	accused
متهم شدن	to be accused
متهم کردن	to accuse
احضار کردن	to summon
احضاریه	summons
اجرا	implementation
اجرا کردن	to implement
استدلال	argumentation
استیناف	appeal
استیناف دادن	to appeal
اقامهٔ دعوی	litigation
اقدام (اقدامات)	measure
بی گناه	innocent

پرونده	case; file
سند (اسناد)	document
مجوّز	permit
مدرک (مدارک)	evidence
ثابت کردن	to prove
تحت ِ تعقیب قرار دادن	to prosecute
تعقیب ِ کیفری	prosecution
تصویب کردن	to ratify
تقاضای طلاق کردن	to file for divorce
رعایت کردن	to abide by
کیفر خواست	indictment
کیفر خواست صادر کردن علیه ِ	to indict
منسوخ کردن	to abolish
نقض کردن	to contravene
واگذاری	settlement
جرم، جنایت (جنایات)	crime
میزان ِ جنایت	crime rate

جنایتکار، مجرم	criminal (n.)
مجرم ِ جنسی	sex offender
جرم شناس	criminologist
جرم شناسی	criminology
جنایی	criminal (adj.)
سابقۀ جنایی	criminal record
خلاف	minor offence
خلافکار، متخلف	offender
خلافکاری	wrongdoing
مرتکب ِ ... شدن	to commit (a crime)
باند ِ تبهکار	criminal gang
قتل ِ عمد	murder
قتل ِ غیر ِ عمد	manslaughter
قتل های زنجیره ای	serial killings
قاتل (قاتلین)	murderer
به قتل رساندن	to murder
تجاوز کردن به	to rape
تخطی	transgression

خشونت ِ خانگی	domestic violence
خیانت	treason
دزد، سارق (سارقین)	thief
دزدی، سرقت	theft
دزدی کردن، سرقت کردن	to steal
قاچاق	smuggling
قاچاقچی	smuggler
قاچاقچی ِ مواد مخدّر	drug smuggler
فروشندهٔ مواد مخدّر	drug dealer
گانگستر	gangster
مافیا	Mafia
آزاد شدن	to be released
آزاد کردن	to release
آزادی ِ مشروط	conditional release
به قید ِ ضمانت آزاد کردن	to release on bail
تبرئه شدن	to be acquitted
اعتراف (اعترافات)	confession
اعتراف کردن	to confess

بازجو	interrogator
بازجویی	interrogation
بازداشت، توقیف	detention
بازداشت ِ حمایتی	protective custody
بازداشت شدن	to be detained
بازداشت شده	detainee
بازداشت کردن	to detain
بازداشتگاه	detention centre
بازرس	inspector
بازرسی	inspection
بررسی	investigation
بررسی کردن	to investigate
پرس و جو	inquiry
تفتیش کردن	to inspect; to search
توقیف کردن	to seize
حبس	confinement
حبس ِ ابد	life imprisonment

حبس ِ انفرادی	solitary confinement
دستگیر شدن	to be arrested
دستگیر کردن	to arrest
دستگیری	arrest
کلانتری	police station
زندان	prison
زندانی	prisoner
زندانی ِ سیاسی	political prisoner
زندانی کردن	to imprison
ضبط ِ اموال	confiscation of property
مصادره کردن	to confiscate
اعدام	execution
اعدام شدن	to be executed
اعدام کردن	to execute
جریمه	fine
جریمه شدن	to be fined

دار زدن	to hang
قدغن کردن	to ban
مجازات	punishment
قابل ِ مجازات	punishable
مجازات شدن	to be punished
مجازات کردن	to punish
مجازات ِ مرگ	capital punishment
ممنوع کردن	to prohibit
ممنوعیت	ban

6. HUMAN RIGHTS

حق (حقوق)	right
حقوق ِ بشر	human rights
نقض ِ حقوق ِ بشر	human rights violation
اعلامیهٔ جهانی ِ حقوق ِ بشر	Universal Declaration of Human Rights
دیده بان ِ حقوق ِ بشر	Human Rights Watch
عفو ِ بین الملل	Amnesty International
حقوق ِ مدنی	civil rights
حقوق ِ همجنسگرایان	gay rights
آزادی	freedom
آزادی ِ اجتماعات	freedom of association
آزادی ِ ادیان	freedom of religion
آزادی ِ بیان	freedom of speech

آزادی ِ مطبوعات	freedom of the press
تبعیض	discrimination
تبعیض آمیز	discriminatory
مورد ِ تبعیض قرار دادن	to discriminate against
تبعیض ِ جنسی	sex discrimination
تبعیض ِ نژادی	racial discrimination
اذیت و آزار	persecution
بردگی	slavery
تجارت ِ انسان	human trafficking
تجاوز	rape
خشونت علیه ِ زنان	violence against women
سانسور	censorship
سانسور کردن	to censor
سوء ِ استفاده	abuse
شکنجه	torture

شكنجه دادن	to torture
شكنجه گر	torturer
نژاد پرست	racist
نژاد پرستی	racism
یهودی ستیزی	anti-Semitism
همجنسگرا ستیزی	homophobia
مهاجرت	immigration; migration
مهاجرت ِ اجباری	forced migration
مهاجر	immigrant
پناه جو	asylum seeker
پناهندگی	asylum
پناهنده	refugee
كميسيون ِ عالی ِ پناهندگان ِ سازمان ِ ملل	UNHCR (United Nations High Commission for Refugees)
غربت	diaspora; exile
تبعید كردن	to exile

7. ECONOMICS

اقتصاد	economics; economy
اقتصادی	economic
بهبود ِ اقتصادی	economic recovery
پیشبینی ِ اقتصادی	economic forecasting
اقتصاددان	economist
اقتصاد ِ بازار ِ آزاد	free market economics
اقتصاد ِ خرد	micro economics
اقتصاد ِ کلان	macro economics
اقتصاد ِ صنعتی	industrial economy
اقتصاد ِ کشاورزی	agrarian economy
اقتصاد ِ معیشتی	subsistence economy
مالی	financial; fiscal
بحران ِ مالی	financial crisis

برنامهٔ نجات ِ مالی	financial rescue package
سال ِ مالی	financial year
محرّک ِ مالی	fiscal stimulus
نظارت ِ مالی	financial regulation
حسابرس	auditor
حسابرسی	auditing
حسابرسی کردن	to audit
تأمین ِ مالی ِ خرد، میکروفاینانس	microfinance
تأمین ِ اجتماعی	social security
بودجه	budget
کسر ِ بودجه	budget deficit
تورّم	inflation
تورّم ِ عنان گسیخته	hyperinflation
تورّم ِ صفر	zero inflation
رشد	growth
رشد ِ منفی	negative growth

رشد کردن	to grow
رکود	recession
دچار ِ رکود، کساد	depressed
سوبسید، یارانه	subsidy
سوبسید دادن به	to subsidise
صرفه جویی کردن	to economise
صندوق	fund
صندوق ِ بازنشستگی	pension fund
کاهش ِ هزینه	spending cut
کلاه برداری	fraud
ارز	foreign currency
ارز ِ قوی	hard currency
ذخیرۀ ارزی	currency reserves
نرخ ِ ارز	exchange rate
پول	currency; money
پولی	monetary
بازار ِ پول	money market
تزریق ِ پول	cash injection

سیستم ِ پولی	monetary system
تبدیل کردن	to change (money)
صرّافی	bureau de change
تضعیف ِ ارزش ِ پول	devaluation
صندوق ِ بین المللی ِ پول	IMF (International Monetary Fund)
حوزهٔ یورو	Eurozone
بانک	bank
شعبه	branch
عابر بانک	ATM (Automated Teller Machine), cashpoint
کارت ِ بانکی	bank card
بانکداری	banking
بانکدار	banker
بانک ِ جهانی	The World Bank
بانک ِ مرکزی	central bank
گروه ِ بانکی	banking group
سیستم ِ بانکداری	banking system

نرخ ِ بانکی	bank rate
نرخ ِ پایه	base rate
پس انداز	savings
حساب	account
حسابدار	accountant
حسابداری	accountancy
اعتبار	credit
بحران ِ اعتبار	credit crunch
خط ِ اعتبار	line of credit
درجهٔ اعتبار	credit rating
کارت ِ اعتباری	credit card
طلبکار	creditor
بدهکار	debtor
بدهکار بودن	to be in debt
بدهی	debt
بدهی ِ ملی	national debt
بهره	interest
بدون ِ بهره	interest-free

نرخ ِ بهره	interest rate
بیعانه، پیش پرداخت	down payment
بازپرداخت	repayment
قسط (اقساط)	instalment
قصور در پرداخت	default
بیمه	insurance
ضامن	guarantor
ضمانت	guarantee
ضمانت کردن	to guarantee
قرض (قروض)	loan
قرض دادن	to loan
قرض گرفتن	to borrow
قرض گیری	borrowing
وام	loan
وام دادن	to loan
وام گرفتن	to take out a loan
وام ِ مسکن	home loan
دارایی، اموال	assets

دارایی های نقدی	liquid assets
سرمایه	capital
سرمایه دار	capitalist
سرمایه داری	capitalism
سرمایه در گردش	floating capital
سرمایه گذار	investor
سرمایه گذاری	investment
سرمایه گذاری کردن	to invest
سود ِ سرمایه	capital gain
مخاطره، ریسک	risk
مخاطره جویی	risk taking
سرمایه گذاری ِ مخاطره آمیز	venture capital
پول ِ نقد	cash
جریان ِ نقدی	cash flow
نقدینگی	liquidity
بازده	yield
درآمد	income

سود	profit
سود بردن از	to profit from
سود ِ خالص	gross profit
سوددهی	profitability
سود ِ ناخالص	net profit
خسارات	losses
ضررده	loss-making
مالیات	tax, taxes
مالیات بندی	taxation
مالیات بر ارث	inheritance tax
مالیات بر ارزش ِ افزوده	value added tax
مالیات بر درآمد	income tax
مالیات ِ خرید	purchase tax
مالیات بستن به	to levy tax on
مالیات دادن	to pay tax
مالیات دهنده	tax payer
اظهارنامهٔ مالیاتی	tax return
بدون ِ مالیات	tax-free

پرهیز از مالیات	tax evasion
پناهگاه ِ مالیاتی	tax haven
تخفیف ِ مالیات	tax relief
سود قبل از مالیات	pre-tax profit
قابل ِ کسر از مالیات	tax-deductible
مشمول ِ مالیات	taxable
معاف از مالیات	tax exempt
ممیّز ِ مالیاتی	tax assessor

8. TRADE & INDUSTRY

بازرگانی، تجارت	commerce; trade
تجارت کردن	to trade
تجارت ِ آزاد	free trade
سازمان ِ تجارت ِ جهانی	WTO (World Trade Organization)
کسری ِ تجاری	trade gap
تجاری، تجارتی	commercial; trade (adj.)
تجاری کردن	to commercialise
علامت ِ تجاری	trademark
مارک	brand
بازرگان، تاجر	merchant; trader
اتاق ِ بازرگانی	chamber of commerce
نمایشگاه ِ تجاری	trade fair
تحریم (تحریمات)	sanction
ممنوعیت ِ خرید و فروش	embargo

ممنوعیت گذاشتن روی ِ	to impose an embargo on
رفع ِ ممنوعیت کردن	to lift an embargo
صادرات	exports
صادر کردن	to export
صادرکننده	exporter
واردات	imports
وارد کردن	to import
واردکننده	importer
گمرک	customs
عوارض	duty; toll
معاف از عوارض ِ گمرکی	duty-free
بار	cargo
با کشتی فرستادن	to ship
بازار	market; bazaar
بازار ِ آزاد	free market
بازار ِ سیاه	black market

بازار ِ کار	job market
بازاری	bazaari
به بازار عرضه کردن	to market
روندهای بازار	market trends
شرایط ِ بازار	market conditions
قیمت ِ بازار	market price
سفارش (سفارشات)	order
سفارش دادن	to order
عرضه و تقاضا	supply and demand
عرضه کردن	to supply
قدرت ِ خرید	buying power
کالا	goods
کالاهای اساسی	commodities
کالاهای مصرفی	consumer goods
اوراق ِ بهادار، سهام	stocks
بورس ِ سهام	stock exchange
دلال ِ سهام	stockbroker
سود ِ سهام	dividend

سهامدار، صاحب ِ سهام	shareholder
سهم ِ متعارف	equity
شاخص	index
مبتنی بر شاخص	index-linked
آگهی	advertisement
آگهی کردن	to advertise
اداره	office; management
اداره کردن	to manage
ادارهٔ مرکزی	head office
مدیر	manager; director
مدیر ِ کل	general manager
مدیر ِ عامل	managing director
مدیریت	management
هیئت ِ مدیره	board
ادغام	merger
انحصار	monopoly
بخش ِ دولتی	state sector
بخش ِ خصوصی	private sector

خصوصی سازی	privatisation
بخش ِ عمومی	public sector
جهانی سازی	globalisation
خرده فروش	retailer
خرده فروشی	retail
عمده فروش	wholesaler
عمده فروشی	wholesale
ارقام ِ فروش	sales figures
رئیس	boss
رقابت	competition
رقابت کردن با	to compete with
رقیب	competitor; rival
شرکت	company
شرکت ِ چند ملیتی	multinational
شرکت ِ سهامی ِ عام با مسئولیت ِ محدود	PLC (private limited company)
شریک (شرکاء)	business partner

کسب و کار	business (field)
تعاونی	cooperative
قرارداد	contract
مشتری	customer
معامله	deal
ملی سازی	nationalisation
ملی کردن	to nationalise
ورشکست شدن	to go bankrupt
ورشکستگی	bankruptcy
هزینه	cost
حرفه	career; profession
حرفه ای	professional
شغل	job
شغل ِ آزاد	self-employment
اشتغال	employment
بیکاری	unemployment
کارفرما	employer
کارگر	worker

کارمند	employee
نیروی کار	work force
همکار	colleague
پیمانکار	contractor
کار آموز	trainee
کار آموزی	training
اتحادیهٔ صنفی	trade union
اتحادیهٔ کارگری	workers' union
روابط ِ کارگر و کارفرما	labour relations
اخراج شدن	to be fired
اخراج کردن	to fire
استخدام شدن	to be hired
استخدام کردن	to employ; to hire
استعفا	resignation
استعفا دادن	to resign
اعتصاب	strike
اعتصاب شکستن	to break a strike

اعتصاب شکن	strike breaker
اعتصاب کردن	to strike
اعتصاب کننده	striker
بازنشستگی	retirement
بازنشسته شدن	to retire
حقوق ِ بازنشستگی	pension
ترفیع	promotion
ترفیع دادن به	to promote
ترفیع گرفتن	to be promoted
تنزیل ِ مرتبه	demotion
حقوق	wage; salary
درآمد	income
معاش	livelihood
حد ِ اقل ِ دستمزد	minimum wage
صنعت (صنایع)	industry
صنعتی	industrial
صنعتی کردن	industrialisation
پسا صنعتی	post-industrial

صنایع ِ تولیدی	manufacturing industry
صنایع ِ سنگین	heavy industry
صنعت ِ توریسم	tourism industry
گردشگری، جهانگردی	tourism
اکوتوریسم	ecotourism
کشاورزی	agriculture
تولید (تولیدات)	production; product
خط ِ تولید	production line
تولید ِ انبوه	mass production
تولید کردن	to produce
تولید کننده	producer
تولید ِ ناخالص ِ داخلی	GDP (Gross Domestic Product)
توزیع	distribution
فرآورده، محصول (محصولات)	product
فرآوردهٔ جنبی	by-product

کمیت	quantity
کیفیت	quality
کنترل ِ کیفی	quality control
ماشینی شدن	mechanisation
مصرف	consumption
مصرفی	consumer (adj.)
جامعهٔ مصرفی	consumer society
مصرف گرایی	consumerism
مصرف کردن	to consume
مصرف کننده	consumer
مواد	materials
مواد ِ خام	raw materials

9. SCIENCE & TECHNOLOGY

علم (علوم)	science
علمی	scientific
دانشمند	scientist
آزمایش	experiment; test
آزمایش کردن	to test
آزمایشگاه	laboratory
آزمایشی، تجربی	experimental
کارشناس	expert
متخصّص (متخصّصین)	specialist
تخصّص	specialisation
مخترع	inventor
اختراع (اختراعات)	invention
اختراع کردن	to invent
اکتشاف (اکتشافات)	discovery
کشف کردن	to discover
پژوهش	research (n.)

پژوهشگر	researcher
تکنولوژی، فنّ آوری	technology
فنّ آوری ِ اطلاعات	IT (information technology)
تکنولوژی ِ زیستی	biotechnology
فنّ آوری ِ سبز	green technology
فنّی	technological
روبات	robot
روبات سازی	robotics
هوش ِ مصنوعی	AI (artificial intelligence)
واقعیت ِ مجازی	virtual reality
رصدخانه	observatory
ستاره	star
ستاره شناس	astronomer
ستاره شناسی	astronomy
سیّاره (سیّارات)	planet
کرۀ زمین	planet earth

کهکشان ِ راه ِ شیری	The Milky Way
کیهان، گیتی	universe
ماهواره	satellite
منظومۀ شمسی	solar system
فضا	space
ایستگاه ِ فضایی	space station
عصر ِ فضا	space age
فضاپیما	spacecraft
فضانورد	astronaut
ابزار	device; gadget
اسکنر، پویشگر	scanner
اسکن کردن، پویش کردن	to scan
پرینتر، چاپگر	printer
پرینت گرفتن، چاپ کردن	to print
مخابرات	telecommunications
تلفن ِ همراه، موبایل	mobile phone
پیامک	text, SMS (Short Message Service)

پیامگیر	answerphone
دستگاه	device
دورنگار	fax
دیجیتالی	digital
کتاب ِ راهنما	manual
گوشی	earpiece
هدفون	headphones
کامپیوتر، رایانه	computer
برنامه نویس	programmer
برنامه نویسی	programming
حافظه	memory
حذف کردن	to delete
داده ها	data
داده پردازی	data processing
ذخیره کردن	to save (e.g. data)
سخت افزار	hardware
نرم افزار	software
سیستم ِ عامل	operating system

صفحهٔ کلید	keyboard
فایل	file
گیگابایت	gigabyte
مگابایت	megabyte
مانیتور	monitor
نصب کردن	to install
وارد کردن	to input
ویروس	virus
آنلاین	online
آپلود	upload
آپلود کردن	to upload
دانلود	download
دانلود کردن	to download
ایمیل، پستِ الکترونیکی	email
اینترنت	internet
اینترنتِ پرسرعت	high-speed internet
کافی نت	internet café
اینترانت	intranet

بی سیم	wireless
پادکست	podcast
رمز ِ عبور	password
سایت	site
وب سایت، پایگاه ِ اینترنتی	website
سرور	server
سرویس دهنده	service provider
شبکه	network
شبکۀ اجتماعی	social networking site
شبکۀ جهانی، وب	worldwide web
صفحه (صفحات)	webpage
صفحۀ اصلی	home page
فیلتر	filter
فیلترشکن	filter breaker
کلیک کردن، فشار دادن	to click
گشت زدن در وب	surfing the web

لینک	link
جستجو کردن	to search (e.g. the web)
موتور ِ جستجو	search engine
وبلاگ	weblog, blog
وبلاگ نویس	blogger
وبلاگ نویسی	blogging

10. ENERGY

انرژی	energy
انرژی ِ اتمی	nuclear energy
رآکتور ِ اتمی	nuclear reactor
غنی سازی ِ اورانیوم	uranium enrichment
زبالۀ اتمی	nuclear waste
پرتوزا	radioactive
پرتوزایی	radioactivity
آژانس ِ بین المللی ِ انرژی ِ اتمی	IAEA (International Atomic Energy Agency)
انرژی ِ جایگزین	alternative energy
انرژی ِ تجدیدپذیر	renewable energy
مصرف ِ انرژی	energy consumption
کارایی انرژی	energy efficiency
انرژی ِ بادی	wind power
توربین ِ بادی	wind turbine

انرژی ِ خورشیدی	solar energy
صفحهٔ خورشیدی	solar panel
انرژی ِ زمین گرمایی	geothermal energy
بازار ِ انرژی	energy market
نیرو	power
نیروی هسته ای	nuclear power
نیروگاه	power station
برق	electricity
برق ِ آبی	hydroelectricity
قطع ِ برق	power cut
ژنراتور	generator
باطری ِ قابل ِ شارژ	rechargeable battery
سوخت	fuel
سوخت ِ فسیلی، سوخت ِ سنگواره ای	fossil fuel
زغال سنگ	coal
گاز	gas

گاز ِ طبیعی	natural gas
منابع ِ طبیعی	natural resources
منابع ِ معدنی	mineral resources
معدن	mine
معدن چی	miner
معدن کاری	mining
نفت	oil
نفت ِ خام	crude oil
نفت خیز	oil-rich
نفت کش	oil tanker
اوپک (سازمان ِ کشورهای صادرکنندهٔ نفت)	OPEC (Organization of the Petroleum Exporting Countries)
بشکه	barrel
بنزین	petrol
بنزین ِ بدون ِ سرب	lead-free petrol
پالایشگاه	refinery

پتروشیمی	petrochemical
چاه ِ نفت	oil well
حفاری	drilling
سکوی حفاری	drilling rig
خط ِ لوله	pipeline
ذخایر ِ نفت	oil reserves
شرکت ِ نفت	oil company
صنعت ِ نفت	oil industry
مخزن ِ نفتی	oil reservoir
میدان ِ نفتی	oilfield
نشت ِ نفت	oil spill
وابسته به نفت	oil-dependent

11. ENVIRONMENT

محیطِ زیست	environment
محیط زیستی	environmental
حفظِ محیطِ زیست	environmental protection
سازگار با محیطِ زیست	environmentally friendly
طرفدارِ محیطِ زیست	environmentalist
فعّالِ محیطِ زیست	environmental activist
اکوسیستم	ecosystem
بوم شناختی	ecological
بوم شناس	ecologist
تداوم پذیری	sustainability
بازیافت	recycling
بازیابی کردن، بازیافتن	to recycle
بازیافتنی، قابلِ بازیافت	recyclable
بازیافته	recycled

زباله	rubbish
قابلِ تجزیهٔ زیست شناختی	biodegradable
طبیعت	nature
طبیعی	natural; organic
آب و هوا، اقلیم	climate
تغییرِ آب و هوا، تغییرِ اقلیم	climate change
اثرِ گلخانه ای	greenhouse effect
گازهای گلخانه ای	greenhouse gases
افزایشِ دمای زمین، گرمایشِ زمین	global warming
بالا آمدنِ سطحِ آبِ دریاها	the rising of sea levels
ذوب شدنِ یخ های قطبی	polar ice cap melting
ردِ پای کربن	carbon footprint
نشرِ کربن	carbon emissions
سوراخِ اوزون	ozone hole
لایهٔ اوزون	ozone layer

آلودگی	pollution
آلودگی ِ هوا	air pollution
مه دود	smog
آلوده	polluted
آلوده کردن	to pollute
رفع ِ آلودگی	decontamination
مادهٔ آلوده کننده	pollutant
انفجار ِ جمعیت	population explosion
رشد ِ جمعیت	population growth
کاهش ِ جمعیت	depopulation
انقراض	extinction
در معرض ِ انقراض	endangered
منقرض	extinct
منقرض شدن	to become extinct
حیات ِ وحش	wildlife
صندوق ِ جهانی ِ حیات ِ وحش	WWF (World-wide Fund for Nature)

بیابان شدن	desertification
جنگل زدایی	deforestation
بلای طبیعی	natural disaster
توفان	storm
توفند	hurricane
خشکسالی، خشکی	drought
ریزش، زمین لغزه	landslide
زلزله، زمین لرزه	earthquake
سونامی	tsunami
سیل	flood
فرسایش	erosion
آتشفشان	volcano
انفجارِ آتشفشانی	volcanic eruption
خاکسترِ آتشفشانی	volcanic ash
ابرِ خاکسترِ آتشفشانی	volcanic ash cloud

12. AID & DEVELOPMENT

امداد، کمک	aid
امدادرسانی، کمک رسانی	relief work
سازمان ِ امدادی	aid organisation
امدادگر	aid worker
داوطلب	volunteer
داوطلبانه	voluntary
سازمان ِ خیریه	charity
سازمان ِ غیر ِ انتفاعی	non-profit organisation
سازمان ِ غیر ِ دولتی	NGO (non-governmental organisation)
اعانه	donation
اهدا کردن	to donate
اهداکننده	donor
بخشیدن ِ قروض	debt cancellation
کمک ِ مالی	financial assistance

انسان دوستانه	humanitarian
بحران ِ انسانی	humanitarian crisis
فاجعه آمیز	catastrophic
پزشکان ِ بدون ِ مرز	MSF (Médecins Sans Frontières)
سازمان ِ جهانی ِ بهداشت	WHO (World Health Organization)
صلیب ِ سرخ	Red Cross
هلال ِ احمر	Red Crescent
میزان ِ موالید	birth rate
میزان ِ مرگ و میر	mortality rate
احتمال ِ طول ِ عمر	life expectancy
تنظیم ِ خانواده	family planning
بیماری ِ مسری	infectious disease
بیماری ِ همه گیر	epidemic
ایدز	AIDS

طاعون	plague
وبا	cholera
بهداری	public health
پیراپزشک	paramedic
درمانگاه	clinic
کمکهای اولیه	first aid
واکسن	vaccine
واکسن زدن به	to vaccinate
فقر	poverty
فقر زده	poverty-stricken
خط ِ فقر	poverty line
تهیدستی	destitution
قحطی	famine
سوء ِ تغذیه	malnutrition
برنامهٔ جهانی ِ غذا	WFP (World Food Programme)
تخریب، ویران سازی	destruction
بازسازی	reconstruction

حلبی آباد	shanty town
پیشرفت	progress
توسعه	development
آژانس ِ توسعه	development agency
توسعه یافته	developed
توسعه نیافته	underdeveloped
در حال ِ توسعه	developing
جهان ِ سوم	third world
غربی شدن	westernisation
مدرن سازی	modernisation
برنامۀ توسعۀ ملل ِ متحد	UNDP (United Nations Development Programme)
آبیاری	irrigation
تصفیۀ آب	water purification
تصفیۀ فاضلاب	waste water treatment

شیرینسازی	desalination
بی سوادی	illiteracy
نهضت ِ سواد آموزی	literacy campaign
امکانات	facilities
زیر بنا	infrastructure

13. CULTURE & SPORT

فرهنگ	culture
فرهنگی	cultural
با فرهنگ	cultured
فرهنگستان ِ زبان و ادب ِ فارسی	Academy of Persian Language and Literature
فرهنگسرا	cultural centre
رایزن ِ فرهنگی	cultural counsellor
سازمان ِ میراث ِ فرهنگی ِ کشور	Iranian Cultural Heritage Organization
آثار ِ میراث ِ جهانی	World Heritage Sites
وزارت ِ فرهنگ و ارشاد ِ اسلامی	Ministry of Culture and Islamic Guidance
اثر (آثار)	work
اثر ِ هنری	work of art

هنر	art
هنری	artistic
هنرهای زیبا	fine arts
هنرهای تجسّمی	plastic arts
هنر ِ اسلامی	Islamic art
هنر ِ معاصر	contemporary art
هنر ِ مفهومی	conceptual art
هنرمند	artist
استودیو	studio
افتتاحیه	opening
نمایشگاه	exhibition
به نمایش گذاشتن	to exhibit
مجموعه	collection
مجموعه دار	collector
جمع کردن	to collect
حراج	auction
گالری	gallery
موزه	museum

موزه دار	museum curator
بیننده	viewer
شنونده	listener
سمعی – بصری	audio-visual
تلویزیون	television
برنامهٔ تلویزیونی	television programme
سریال ِ تلویزیونی	television series
رادیو	radio
تئاتر	theatre
سن	stage
صحنه	scene; stage
نمایش نامه	play
نمایش نامه نویس	playwright
درام	drama
تراژدی	tragedy
کمدی	comedy
سینما	cinema

فیلم	film
فیلمساز	film-maker
کارگردان	director
فیلمبرداری	filming
فیلم ِ مستند	documentary
جشنوارۀ فیلم	film festival
جایزه (جوایز)	prize
هنرپیشه	actor
ستاره	star
شهرت	fame
عکاس	photographer
عکاسی	photography
منتقد (منتقدین)	critic
خاطرات	memoir
رمان	novel
رمان نویس	novelist
شاعر (شعراء)	poet
شعر (اشعار)	poetry; lyrics

شعر خوانی	poetry reading
شب ِ شعر	poetry evening
نویسنده	writer
کانون ِ نویسندگان ِ ایران	Iranian Writers' Association
کتاب ِ پرفروش	best seller
نقد ِ کتاب	book review
موسیقی	music
موسیقی ِ پاپ	pop music
موسیقی ِ سنتی	traditional music
آلت ِ موسیقی، ساز	musical instrument
نوازنده، موزیسین	musician
نواختن، زدن	to play
آلبوم	album
سی دی	CD
ضبط کردن	to record
آهنگ	song
آهنگ ساز	composer

خواننده	singer
اپرا	opera
رپ ِ فارسی	Persian rap
اجرا	performance
اجرا کردن	to perform
ارکستر	orchestra
رهبر ِ ارکستر	conductor
استاد	maestro
کنسرت	concert
تالار ِ کنسرت	concert hall
ورزش	sport
ورزشکار	sportsperson; sporty (adj.)
ورزشگاه	sports club
باشگاه	club
بازی	game
بازی های المپیک	Olympic Games
بازی کردن	to play

بازیکن	player
بردن	to win
برنده	winner
باختن	to lose
بازنده	loser
تقلب کردن	to cheat
مسابقه (مسابقات)	competition; match
مسابقهٔ حذفی	qualifier
راه یافتن به	to qualify
دورِ نیمه نهایی	semi-final
فینال، بازیِ نهایی	final
قهرمان	champion
قهرمانی	championship
جامِ جهانی	The World Cup
لیگ	league
امتیاز (امتیازات)	point; score
مدال	medal
استادیوم	stadium

زمین ِ تنیس	tennis court
زمین ِ فوتبال	football pitch
تیم ِ ملی	national team
کاپیتان	captain
داور	referee
فوتبالیست، بازیکن ِ فوتبال	football player
گل زدن	to score a goal
پنالتی	penalty
تماشاچی، تماشاگر	spectator
طرفدار	supporter
مربّی	coach

INDEX